S0-BMZ-418

# SIGN
# LANGUAGE
# TALK

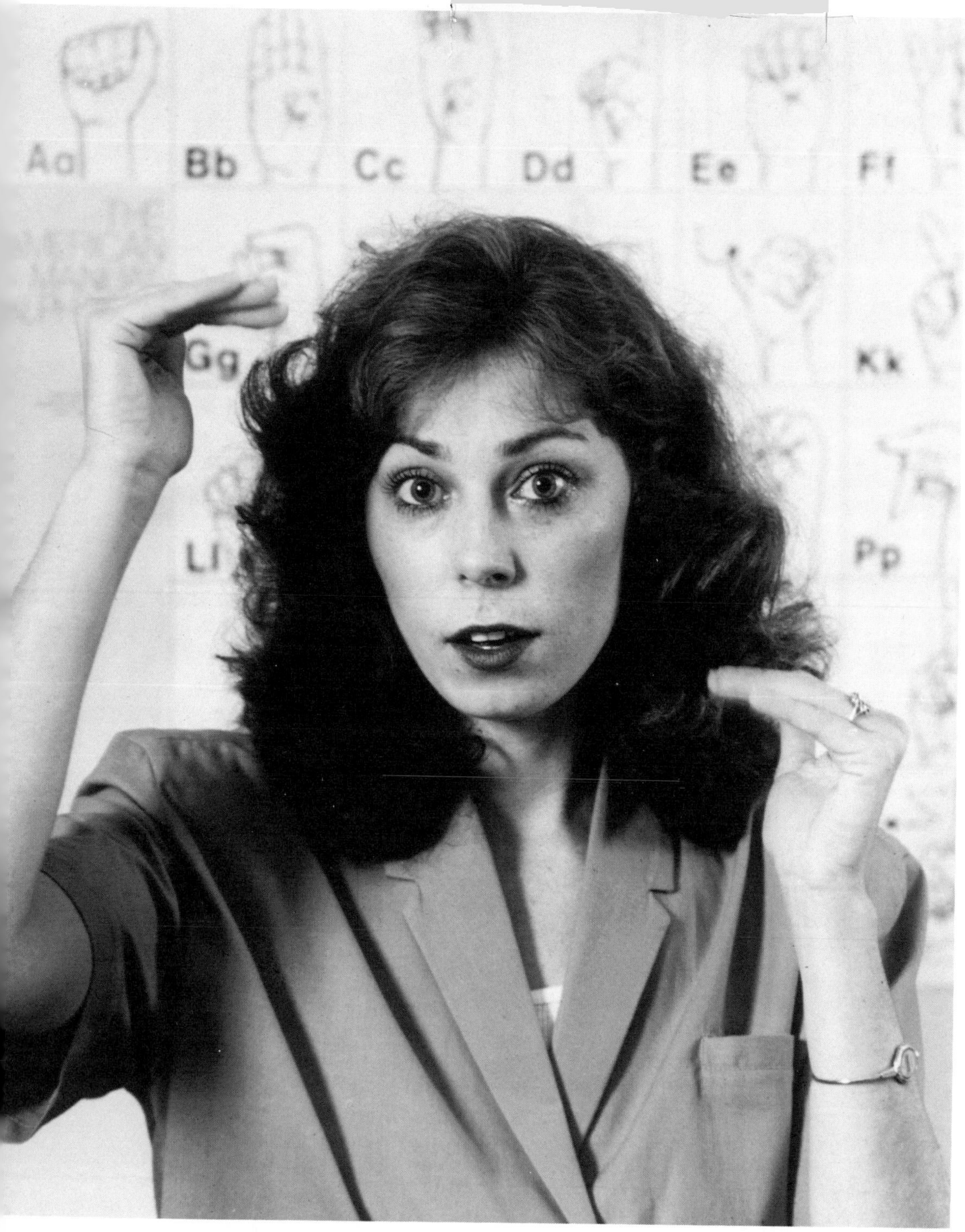
Aa
Bb
Cc
Dd
Ee
Ff
Gg
Kk
Pp

# SIGN LANGUAGE TALK

**by Laura Greene
and Eva Barash Dicker**

A FIRST BOOK
FRANKLIN WATTS
NEW YORK/LONDON/TORONTO
SYDNEY/1989

Frontis: *a woman signs for the deaf
with a sign alphabet chart behind her.*

Library of Congress Cataloging-in-Publication Data

Greene, Laura.
Sign language talk / by Laura Greene and Eva Barash Dicker.
p.  cm. —
Bibliography: p.
Includes index.
Summary: Examines the fundamental differences between written and
spoken English and American Sign Language, the first language for
more than 250,000 deaf people in North America. Includes
instructions for using sign language in playing games, reading
poetry, and singing songs.
ISBN 0-531-10597-0
1. Sign language—Juvenile literature.  2. Deaf—Means of
communication—Juvenile literature.  [1. Sign language.  2. Deaf
3. Physically handicapped.]  I. Dicker, Eva Barash.  II. Title.
III. Series.
HV2476.G735  1989
419—dc19                                             88-5617
                                                       CIP
                                                        AC

Cover art by Anne Canevari Green
Interior illustrations copyright © by Caren Caraway

*Language is the key to
understanding people.
This book is dedicated
to those who try to
understand the shapes
and sounds of language.*

# Contents

# 1

# Some Background

## AMERICAN SIGN LANGUAGE

American Sign Language (often called Ameslan or ASL) is the sign language used by most deaf people in the United States and Canada. It differs from other sign languages as much as English differs from other spoken languages. ASL is the first language for approximately 250,000 to 500,000 deaf people living in North America.

Although many people believe that ASL is a more natural language for deaf children in an English-speaking culture than spoken English, deaf children spend more time in school learning the rules of spoken and written English than they spend on any other subject. This is because it is widely believed that even though a person is deaf, he or she ought to be able to communicate in the language of the majority. Most deaf children do not even formally study ASL grammar in school.

Most people learn their native language from their parents. However, since 90 percent of all deaf children are born to hearing parents, deaf children pick up their knowledge of ASL from their deaf peers, deaf adults other than their parents, or non-native speakers, and they gain their language skills at a much later age than hearing children. All this makes language learning extremely difficult.

DEAF

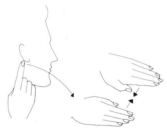

Right index finger touches right ear.
Palms face down,
then forefingers touch.

SCHOOL

Hands are clapped twice
with left palm up.

9

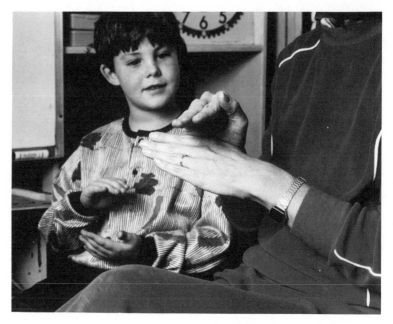

*This Harrisburg, Pennsylvania, primary-grade deaf student tries to copy his teacher's movements and handshapes.*

TOMORROW

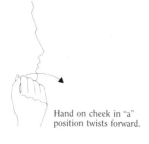

Hand on cheek in "a" position twists forward.

TIME

Right index finger taps top of left wrist.

The problems increase because the grammatical structures of English and ASL are quite different. For example, English uses parts of speech called articles, such as *a, an,* and *the.* ASL does not use these. English has a system of verb tenses to indicate whether an action *took* place (past tense), *is taking* place (present tense), or *will take* place (future tense). ASL can communicate the same concepts but does not use tense to do so. Instead, it uses specific signs to indicate when something has taken or will take place. Signs for LONG-AGO or TOMORROW designate a time in the past or future. (Note that words in this book printed in all capital letters are meant to represent the closest English words to existing ASL signs. And when two capitalized words are hyphenated, it means that the signer makes a single sign to indicate both words. These are customary practices when writing about ASL.)

This brings up another important point, which is that neither English nor ASL can be translated word for word into the other. If you have begun studying a foreign language, you will realize how difficult it is to accurately translate any language into another. With all but the simplest of sentences and ideas, it is almost impossible to convey the exact meaning. Some

10

words cannot be translated at all. A language is more than words. It is culture as well. This is one reason why people of different cultures can so easily misunderstand one another.

Since sign language words represent concepts and not spoken English words, a single ASL sign can be translated into any number of different English words. For example, one ASL sign represents all of these spoken English words: *friendly, sociable, pleasant, hospitable,* or *agreeable.* Although these English words are all synonyms (similar in meaning to each other), they do not mean *exactly* the same thing. Thus, even if an English word is conveyed by a sign, the sign may not carry the full meaning intended. Often the result is misinterpretation. We will try to avoid any misinterpretation here and be satisfied with the closest translation we can get, even if it is not enough.

NOT

## SPOKEN LANGUAGES VS. GESTURAL LANGUAGES

A hearing-impaired person can dream in sign language, mutter quietly in sign language, and even giggle over finger fumblers the way hearing people giggle over tongue twisters. Parents have seen their deaf children sign themselves to sleep and watched them hold imaginary signing conversations with their dolls and stuffed animals. A deaf child whose parents are also deaf develops sign language by first making nonsense gestures, just the way a hearing child learns to talk by first babbling nonsense sounds.

SLEEP

Open palm is placed in front of face. Hands move down as fingers close.

There are many different signing styles and regional variations within sign languages, just as there are numerous accents and regional differences within spoken languages. Sign languages can communicate all the emotions and ideas that any spoken language can. In other words, sign languages are sophisticated communications systems designed to meet the special needs of the deaf. Like all natural languages, sign languages develop naturally when people who have a common bond, and a common culture, wish to communicate with one another.

In all languages, whether spoken or visual, there is room for individuality, creativity, and self-expression. Just as most hearing people sometimes speak excitedly and sometimes

HEARING

Index finger moves out from mouth, in corkscrew motion.

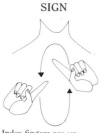

SIGN

Index fingers are up, with palms out. Hands move in alternate circles.

mumble, so, too, deaf people sometimes sign dramatically or are sometimes unclear.

The words "sign language" refer to all the visual, or gestural, languages used throughout the world. Any language, whether spoken or visual, has its own unique symbol system, formal structure, and rules of grammar. Sign languages in general, however, have one thing in common that spoken languages do not. They all require the use of body language and facial expressions to convey meaning. The hands, face, eyes, arms, body posture, and space around the body are essential to the communication system. Movements of the body and face occur according to specific language rules, just as consonants and vowels are arranged in a spoken language.

*The National Theatre of the Deaf performing* My Third Eye. *Note the dramatic facial expressions and body movements accompanying the handshapes.*

Gestural languages are unique in that they are structured to fit the needs and capabilities of the eyes rather than the ears. A slight difference in the position of a finger, an expression on the face, or the speed of a sign can change the meaning of a word or thought. Deaf people communicate over light waves just as hearing people communicate over sound waves. One method is not better or worse than the other, only different.

In spoken languages the message-giver is the speaker. The speaker knows how to use his or her lips, tongue, teeth, and the rest of the vocal apparatus to make oral sounds the listener will understand. The word "pat," for example, requires that the speaker use lips, tongue, and vocal chords in a way quite different than if he or she were saying the word "whale." The receiver of these sounds uses the ears (aural organs) to hear the sounds that carry the meaning of the message. Spoken language is, therefore, both oral and aural. In sign language, the message-giver makes gestures and uses facial expressions and body movements to convey meaning. The message-receiver uses the eyes (visual organs) to see the signs and facial expressions that carry this meaning. The language, therefore, is both gestural and visual: gestural on the part of the giver and visual on the part of the receiver.

ASL requires many skills that a spoken language does not. For example, in ASL it is the face that tells the message-receiver if the speaker is mildly happy, very happy, or "I'm so happy I could fly." The speed of the hand or fingers conveys the idea of exactly how fast a person walked to school. Was it at an ordinary pace or a leisurely stroll? Did the person walk quickly because of excitement or because he or she was being chased? Although facial expressions and hand movements often accompany spoken languages, they are not as essential in spoken languages as they are in gestural languages. A single sign plus accompanying body movements and facial expressions can easily serve as a complete statement, or carry the meaning of several English words. An expression on the face or the speed of a movement can mean a great deal. By themselves, parts of signs, like parts of words, are meaningless; but when put together they convey a great deal of information.

The ability of slight variations in sound to carry different meanings is an important factor in spoken languages. Replacing one vowel in a word, for example, produces a brand-new

FACE

Right index finger moves clockwise around the face.

SEE

"V" position on right hand touches side of right eye and moves away from face.

PUT

Both hands, fingers together, move in any direction.

13

word, as in "bet" and "bit" or "pot" and "put." In sign languages slight variations in the movement or shape of the hand are equally significant.

In a spoken language differences in vocal emphasis may dramatically change the meaning of a sentence. For example, the questions "May I *go*?" and "May *I* go?" mean different things. The first means that the speaker is being detained and doesn't want to be. The emphasis on "go" expresses anger or annoyance. The second sentence means that the speaker is eager to go either instead of someone else or in addition to someone else. There is no anger implied. Thus, communication in a spoken language is carried not only by the words themselves but also by *emphasis*.

Emphasis can change meaning in a visual language, too. In ASL, emphasis gives the original sign a sense of urgency. For example, the sign for WANT, when emphasized, becomes REALLY-WANT; HUNGRY becomes VERY-HUNGRY; and SIT becomes the command SIT-DOWN. To emphasize a sign in ASL the signer will not only sign forcefully, but his or her face will also express urgency.

It is difficult to translate emphasis and tone of voice in a spoken language into the signs of a gestural language. It is equally difficult to translate forceful signs and expressions into spoken words.

## INVENTED LANGUAGES

Over the years, teachers in the United States have worked hard to make English easier for deaf children to learn. To do this they have devised codes made up of existing ASL signs and invented symbols for words or word parts that are not in ASL; all this is then put into English-language order.

Coded communications are not natural languages. In fact, they are not languages at all. They are instead invented systems that are superimposed on other languages. In other words, they are *adaptations* of an existing language.

The various invented communications systems fall into several different groups that are either more or less similar to spoken English. These systems are called *manually coded English* (MCE).

Deaf people have had great difficulty learning these systems. First of all, no code can adequately represent a language;

WORD

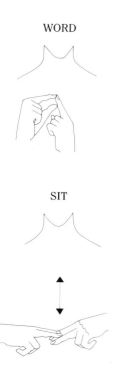

SIT

CHILDREN

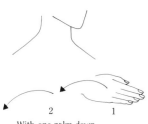

With one palm down, right hand moves as if to pat top of child's head. Repeat motion to side to indicate more than one child.

second, the various code-makers did not accept each other's ideas; and third, even though many adults learned a coded system as children, most did not fully adopt any of the codes as their system of daily communication. ASL was more natural for conversation. Therefore, they preferred it for communication among themselves.

However, the effort to make English understandable through codes did influence American Sign Language. For example, in one code the word for "family" is fingerspelled. The ASL sign for "family" used to be made with cupped hands. Now, however, in order to sign the word "family," the hands are first shaped into the letter "f."

FAMILY

Both hands in "f" position make circle moving downward in front of body.

## PSE

One of the most significant results of adapting the needs of one culture to the needs of another was the development of *pidgin sign English* (PSE). Pidgin languages are systems that develop naturally when people who do not know each other's language want to communicate. They typically combine the vocabulary and structure of both languages but follow the grammar of one. When hearing people and deaf people wish to communicate with each other they will generally use PSE, a "compromise" language. (Relatively few hearing people ever even get the opportunity to learn pure ASL.)

Although ASL is considered the more natural language of the majority of deaf people, a significant number of deaf people use PSE exclusively. ASL and PSE use the same signs. However, PSE more or less follows English word order, while ASL uses its own unique system of word order. The chart at the end of this chapter will show the relationship between English, PSE, and ASL. It's called a *language continuum*. It shows that English and ASL are two different languages and that there are a variety of adaptations of both languages in between.

FRIEND

Index fingers lock. Hands switch position and repeat motion.

## LEARNING ASL

Many people already know a little pidgin sign. Maybe you have read about the history and development of ASL and have taken the time to learn the fingerspelling handshapes. It helps to know these things. It also helps if you know the shapes of a few signs and have practiced them with your friends in sign

15

# THE MANUAL ALPHABET

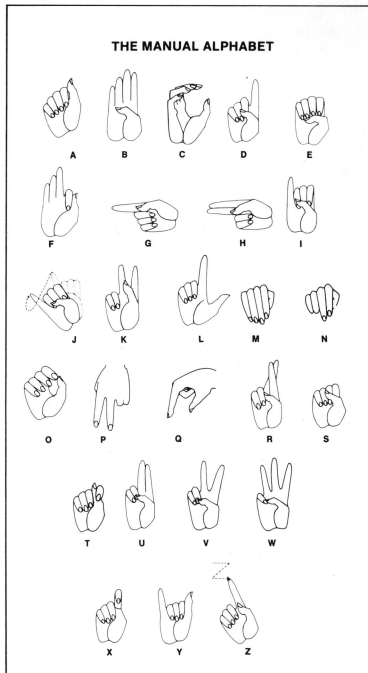

language games (see the book *Sign Language* [Watts; 1981], also by Laura Greene and Eva Barash Dicker). Knowing all these things is the first step in learning ASL. However, to really communicate in a language, a person must learn a great deal more than the alphabet and a few vocabulary words.

The object of this book is to provide the second step in language learning by showing you how grammatically correct ASL sentences are formed. You will also learn how to express feelings and ideas in poetry and song. To become truly fluent in any language, however, you will need lots of practice and ultimately some formal training with a teacher.

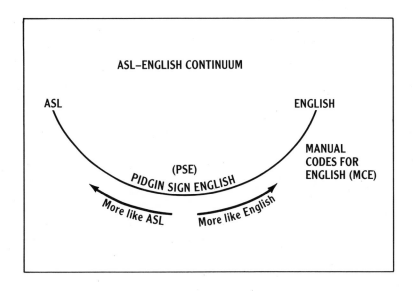

# 2

# Taking It Apart: ASL Building Blocks

## BUILDING BLOCKS

All languages are made up of meaningless symbols called *building blocks.* In spoken languages one of these building blocks is sound. Minor changes in sound are very important. For example, you can take your "pet" for a walk but not your "pot." A single sound means a lot. Sounds added to a word also change its meaning. Add an "s" to "pet" and you get "pets." In this example "s" means more than one. Add an "un" to "happy" and you get "unhappy." A "pet" might make you "happy," but "pets" might make your parents "unhappy." Additions to a word change meaning.

In English, but not in all spoken languages, another building block is word order. The sentence "Roscoe poked Nestor" means something quite different from "Nestor poked Roscoe." The sounds are identical, but the order changes the meaning. In some languages word order is not important. There is no right or wrong way to combine sounds or words to form meaning; people simply agree on a system and then follow it.

American Sign Language, like other languages, is made up of separate elements or building blocks. These elements interact and combine with each other in a certain agreed-upon or-

HAPPY

Chest is patted several times with upward motion.

18

*Students at Gallaudet University, a school for the deaf, converse in sign language. The student in the picture is signing the letter "e."*

der. ASL is *not* signed English; it has its own structure and its own grammar. By examining the building blocks of ASL we will see how it is different from spoken English. The rules in spoken English help us to decide when to say which sounds and how to combine those sounds. Similarly, the rules in ASL help us to decide how to combine parts of signs to form meaning. The parts of signs are:

DIFFERENT

Index fingers touch on sides, then pull apart.

1. handshapes (the way the hands are shaped);
2. movements (the way the hands are moved);
3. locations of signs (where the hands are located in relation to the signer's body); and
4. palm orientation (the direction the palms face).

Also, as we indicated earlier, since many sign words stand for ideas or concepts, a number of spoken English words may be required to express the full meaning of one sign. In the reverse, a spoken word may require a number of signs to convey its fullest meaning in ASL.

The parts of sign formation are as essential to ASL as sound formation is to English. Small differences mean a great deal. Here are some examples to help you understand the parts. Remember, when you see a word in this book written in CAPITAL LETTERS, it means that it is the spoken English word closest in meaning to an ASL sign.

*Handshape*

In ASL the difference between the word signs WHITE and LIKE is very small. The two words differ only in the handshape. WHITE uses all the fingers, while LIKE uses only the thumb and middle finger.

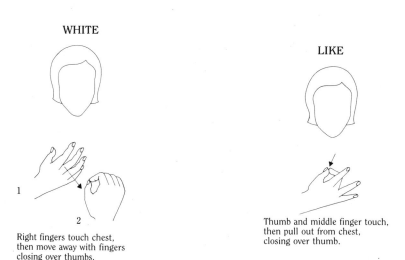

WHITE

LIKE

1

2

Right fingers touch chest, then move away with fingers closing over thumbs.

Thumb and middle finger touch, then pull out from chest, closing over thumb.

The location (on the chest), the movement of the sign (out from the chest), and the orientation of the palm (facing the body), however, are the same in both signs. The hand is positioned on the chest, the palm faces toward the body, and the movement is away from the body. (It doesn't matter which hand is used. Most signers, as most people, are right-handed and therefore make one-handed signs with their right or dominant hand. When two hands are needed it is the right one that moves. Left-handed people make one-handed signs with their left hand and in two-handed signs move their left hand. The artwork in this book will show a right-handed signer.)

## Movement

The difference between MOTHER and GRANDMOTHER is movement. In both words the five fingers of either hand are spread open, the thumb is on the chin, and the palm faces the left. But while the hand remains relatively still in MOTHER, there is some movement away from the chin in GRANDMOTHER.

MOTHER

Thumb touches chin.

GRANDMOTHER

With thumb on chin, hand moves outward.

## Location

The difference between the sign for FATHER and the sign for MOTHER is in the location. An open hand with the thumb placed on the chin means MOTHER. An open hand with the thumb placed on the forehead means FATHER. The handshape, movement, and palm orientation are the same for MOTHER and FATHER.

FATHER

Right thumb touches forehead, then fingers wiggle.

## Palm Orientation

The signs for NAME and SIT use different palm orientations. In SIT the palm faces down, while in NAME the palm faces the left. Everything else is the same.

NAME

Two fingers of right hand tap two fingers of left hand.

SIT

21

# LET'S PRACTICE

Look at these signs. Think about what makes each sign differ from the other. Is it handshape? Is it movement? Is it location? Is it palm orientation? The answers appear on page 25.

### 1. sit

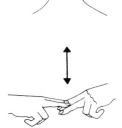

### name

Two fingers of right hand tap two fingers of left hand.

### 2. year

Closed right hand circles around left fist, then rests there.

### world

Both hands form "w" shape. Right hand circles around left, then rests there.

### 3. child

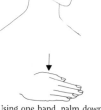

Using one hand, palm down, move hand as if to pat the top of a child's head.

### adult

Hold hand steady above head.

## 4. father

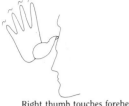

Right thumb touches forehead,
then fingers wiggle.

## mother

Thumb touches chin.

## 5. chocolate

"C" position on right hand circles
on top of left fist.

## church

"C" position on right hand repeatedly
taps top of left fist.

## 6. red

Index finger is pulled down over lips.

## pink

Middle finger in "p" position
is pulled down over lips.

### 7. onion

Twist knuckle.

### apple

Twist knuckle.

### 8. wonderful

Hands move rapidly
forward and back.

### Sunday

Circle both hands in
opposite directions.

### 9. open

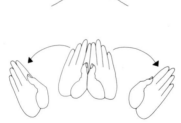

### close

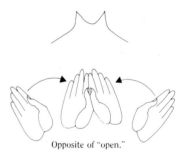

Opposite of "open."

### 10. butter

Repeat motion several times.

### paint

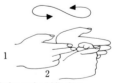

1

2

Index and middle finger
on right hand brush left hand
palm open, in painting motion—in
and out, back and forth.

## 11. white

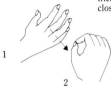

Right fingers touch chest,
then move away with fingers
closing over thumbs.

1

2

## like

Thumb and middle finger touch,
then pull out from chest,
closing over thumb.

## 12. appointment

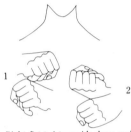

Right fist circles and rests
on back of left fist.

## lock

1

2

Right fist twists upside down and
rests on top of left fist.

## SIGN SPACE

In addition to the building blocks of sign formation, another important part of the ASL system is the use of space. When using ASL a signer must be able to use the space in front of him or her in a very special way. That space is called *sign space*. Sign space is also important for grammar. It is the proper use of sign space (rather than word order) that indicates "Rosco poked Nestor," and not the other way around.

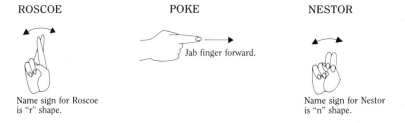

ROSCOE

POKE

NESTOR

Jab finger forward.

Name sign for Roscoe is "r" shape.

Name sign for Nestor is "n" shape.

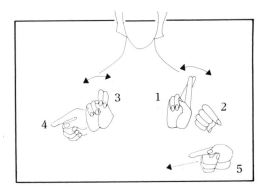

Since a receiver looks primarily at the face, most signs are made in the area just below the face, head, and neck. Signs that are made in the chest and waist area are often two-handed.

Sign space is the area from the top of the head to just below the waist. This space forms an imaginary rectangle in front of the signer. Signers may use more or less space just as speakers may use soft or loud voices. A few signs require the use of the space above the head, as in BASKETBALL, or below the waist, as in GOLF.

BASKETBALL

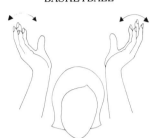

Both hands throw imaginary basketball over head.

GOLF

Clasp hands as if holding a golfclub.

## INDEXING

*Indexing* is a sign language shortcut. It is a method that allows the signer to create a visual picture of action and relationships between people or objects without unnecessary repetition.

Indexing takes just two steps:

1. Establish a specific location within the sign space for each person or object involved. Be certain that each person or object has a different spot.
2. Refer to each person or object again and again by pointing with the index finger to the designated spot within the sign space.

INDEXING

A signer may use indexing whenever it is necessary to refer to a person, place, or thing more than once.

## NONMANUAL ASPECTS

A significant part of sign language is the *nonmanual component.* In ASL there are certain head, eye, lip, and body movements that add meaning. Proper use of the face and body are necessary for fluent communication. For example, nonmanual behavior alerts the observer as to whether the sentence will be a question, a simple statement, a negative statement, or a conditional statement. In the question "Do you scuba dive?", the

27

signer will sign SCUBA DIVE, YOU? and will raise the eyebrows and tilt the head or sometimes the whole body forward. This nonmanual behavior indicates that a question is being asked. To answer the question negatively and say, "No one around here scuba dives," the signer may shake the head from side to side, frown, and make accompanying signs.

NO ONE

Both hands in "o" position move
at an angle away from the body.
Right hand ends with index finger up,
palm facing in.
Head moves side to side also.

DIVES

Both hands over head move
down in diving motion.

Conditional sentences also require specific body movements. A conditional sentence has two parts: the *condition* ("If the stable is not too far") and the *result* ("maybe my mother will drive me"). In English, either part may come first. In ASL, the condition must be signed *before* the result. The conditional part of the sentence requires that the eyebrow be raised and the head and the body slightly tilted. As the result is signed, the signer shifts the body to indicate that what follows will be a simple statement.

In addition to whole sentences having a nonmanual aspect, words and phrases may also be accompanied by nonmanual movement. For example, when the lips are pursed, that is, shaped as though one were about to whistle, it indicates that the signed object is very small, thin, narrow, or smooth. When the jaw drops as if to say "cha," or the cheeks are puffed, the idea is "huge," "big," or "large."

## LET'S PRACTICE

The nonmanual aspects of ASL are as important as the manual aspects. Look at the pictures below and see if you can identify the nonmanual aspects. What additional information does each one give you? The answers appear below.

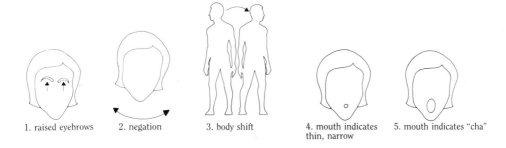

1. raised eyebrows     2. negation     3. body shift     4. mouth indicates thin, narrow     5. mouth indicates "cha"

## LET'S REVIEW

In this chapter we have examined some of the building blocks of ASL. We have seen how a sign is made of four parts: hand-shape, movement, location, and palm orientation. These parts combine and interact with each other in sign space. Sign space is the area in front and to either side of the signer. It is where signers place their signs.

In addition to the manual aspects (hand motions) of sign language, ASL relies heavily on nonmanual communication, that is, the use of the face and the body. These nonmanual aspects are essential for fluent communication. In the next chapter we will put all the parts together as we discuss sentence building and the grammar of ASL.

*Answers:*
1. Raised eyebrows indicate a question.
2. Head shaking indicates "no."
3. Body shift indicates a conditional sentence.
4. Pursed lips indicate something small.
5. Open mouth indicates something big.

# 3

# Putting It Together: ASL Grammar

Neither sounds nor shapes, words nor signs are enough to make language. A language is made up of words that can be organized to form meaningful sentences. There are many different methods that enable people to express what is, what was, what might be, and what will be. Each language has its own way of showing time, condition, relationships, negation, and so on. In this chapter we will examine the way ASL combines signs to form sentences.

## WORD ORDER

Word order is one important way in which languages vary. English, for example, requires that an adjective, a word that describes a noun, precede the noun. We say "green shoes," not "shoes green." In ASL, however, the adjective almost always *follows* the noun. For example, an ASL signer who wanted to communicate the idea that the short, plump girl is beautiful would sign the noun (girl) first, index it in the sign space, and follow it with the description (short, plump, beautiful). Thus,

## GIRL (INDEX)

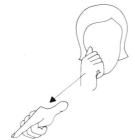

"A" position on right hand brushes
down gently against right cheek
and points to imaginary girl.

## SHORT

## PLUMP

Cheeks puff out. Hands in claw shape
move out from cheeks.

## BEAUTIFUL

Hand with fingers open circle in front of face,
then fingers close.

GIRL (index) SHORT PLUMP BEAUTIFUL is preferred to SHORT PLUMP BEAUTIFUL GIRL.

In complete simple sentences, English usually follows a subject-verb-object word order. For example, in English we say: "Girls ride horses." If we say "Horses ride girls," we will be making grammatical sense but no sense otherwise. It is the word order that tells us who or what did the riding and who or what was ridden. In a language such as Latin, however, it

## HORSES

With thumb touching temple
and two fingers together,
hand moves up and down.

## RIDE

Right hand in "v" position
straddles left forefinger.
Both hands move forward.

31

doesn't matter which word is said first. These Latin sentences both mean "Girls ride horses":

*Puellae equitant.*
*Equitant puellae.*

*Puellae* has an "ae" at the end, which is a *case ending.* The case ending tells us who does the action—"girls."

ASL word order is not like English word order, nor does it follow the Latin case-ending strategy. In ASL, the major idea is signed first. If the signer thinks "horses" is the major idea, then HORSES will be signed first. If the signer thinks "girls" is the major idea, GIRLS will be signed first.

*Teens practice the sign language alphabet.*

## REPETITION

When a sign is repeated it carries more meaning. For example, in the sentence, "That game is really fun," if the sign REALLY is repeated, the signer means that the activity is not just ordinary fun but something quite special.

A signer may also repeat a word to indicate that he or she does something regularly. In the sentence, "On Saturday afternoons I carpool with a friend," the word SATURDAY will be repeated if carpooling is a regular activity on Saturdays. If the signer wants to indicate that he or she has been horseback riding for years, the sign YEARS will be repeated. This is one way to indicate an ongoing activity.

Sometimes a sign can be either a noun or a verb. This is called a *noun-verb pair.* Repetition of that sign indicates whether it is a noun or a verb. For example, the sign for AIRPLANE and FLY have the same handshape, location, movement, and palm orientation. However, the noun AIRPLANE is signed by repeating the movement, while with the verb FLY the movement is made only once.

Repetition of a sign can have two additional purposes in ASL. First, it can make a word or an action plural; and second, if a sign is made slowly and repeatedly, it means that the task required a long time to finish. For example, if the sign for WORK is repeated, it means hard work or time-consuming work. Of course, all signs must be done with appropriate facial expressions. Otherwise, the reason for the repetition will be unclear.

## NEGATION

If a group of friends are communicating in spoken English and someone suggests that they all go out for hot dogs, someone might say, "I don't like hot dogs."

On the other hand, if a group of friends are communicating in ASL and one of them doesn't like hot dogs, that person would sign HOT-DOGS LIKE ME but negate the sign by shaking his or her head from side to side and giving other nonmanual indicators. However, there is a sign for NOT that could be used instead of, or in addition to, the headshake.

In English, as well as in ASL, there are a variety of ways to negate sentences. For example, in English it would be cor-

**YEARS**

Closed right hand circles around left fist. Repeat several times.

**AIRPLANE**

Fingers jab forward and back.

**FLY**

Fingers jab forward and back.

**HOT DOGS**

Hands in "c" position, sides touching, move away from each other as fingers close.

rect to say, "I don't own a horse," and incorrect to say, "Horse none me." In ASL, however, the sentence HORSE NONE ME is grammatically correct. The word order of I DON'T OWN A HORSE is incorrect in ASL.

NONE

Hands with fingers in "o" position
move away from each other.

The verbs HAVE, SEE, UNDERSTAND, FEEL, HEAR, EAT, and GET are frequently negated with the sign for NONE. The NONE sign is also used to mean "zero." The English sentence: "I haven't any friends yet" is signed FRIENDS NONE ME NOT YET.

ME                                        NOT YET

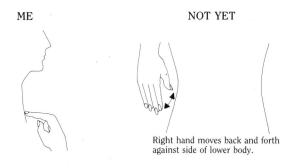

Right hand moves back and forth
against side of lower body.

ASL has grammatical rules for negation, but they are not the same as English rules. In ASL, a negative sign such as DON'T, NOT, or CAN'T may be put either before the verb or at the end of the sentence. If it's put at the end, or repeated at the end, the emphasis is greater.

Sometimes ideas are negated with a twisting hand motion or by reversing the order of the sign. Examples of such words are:

WANT

DON'T-WANT

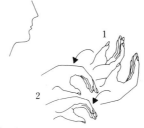

Both hands in claw position, palms up, move toward body.

Both hands start in claw position, palms up. Hands then twist upside down.

WITH

WITHOUT

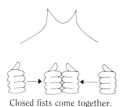

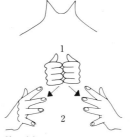

Closed fists come together.

Closed fists touch, then move away from each other, opening.

KNOW

DON'T-KNOW

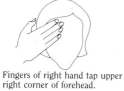

Fingers of right hand tap upper right corner of forehead.

In English, we sometimes reverse meaning by adding the prefix "un," as in do/undo; cover/uncover; forget/unforgettable. In ASL, when negative words are used, they are sometimes accompanied by side-to-side head shaking and perhaps a frown, knitted brows, and wrinkling of the nose.

35

# LET'S PRACTICE

1. In the sentences below, see if you can figure out what would be signed first. Do you know why?

   a. This candy tastes sweet.

CANDY

Index and middle fingers on right hand touch chin and move down.

SWEET

All fingers on right hand except thumb touch chin and move down.

   b. We use umbrellas in the rain.
   c. I love hot dogs.

2. There are three different ways to sign "This candy is not sweet." Describe them.

UMBRELLAS

Right fist moves up and down as if opening and closing an umbrella.

*Answers:*

1a. CANDY, because it is the main idea.
1b. UMBRELLAS, because it is the main idea.
1c. HOT DOGS, because it is the main idea.
2. The three ways are:
a. Shake your head from side to side while signing the sentence.
b. Sign CANDY SWEET NOT or CANDY SWEET NO.

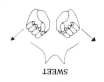

SWEET          NO

c. Sign CANDY NOT SWEET while shaking your head from side to side and frowning.

There are several correct ways to sign the same thing in ASL, just as there are several ways to say the same thing in English. It is the message-giver who decides the full meaning of the message.

## TENSE

Every language must have a way to indicate tense, that is, whether an action is taking place now (present tense), took place in the past (past tense), or will take place in the future (future tense). In English, tense is indicated by changing the form of the verb. For example, we have: *freeze, froze, frozen, will freeze, will have frozen, had frozen, can be frozen, might have been frozen,* and so on. ASL does not change the form of the verb to indicate time. Instead, signers use *time words*. Time words are placed at or near the beginning or the end of the unit of communication. Although English also has time words, they are not as essential as they are in ASL.

|  English | ASL |
|---|---|

I am going horseback riding today.     TODAY HORSE RIDE ME

TODAY

With both hands at right angles, palms up, index finger of right hand moves to left to rest on left arm.

37

**YESTERDAY**

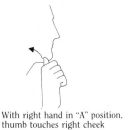

With right hand in "A" position, thumb touches right cheek and moves back.

I went horseback riding.
(The words *yesterday, long ago,* or *recent[ly]* are not required in English.)

YESTERDAY HORSE RIDE ME
LONG-AGO HORSE RIDE ME
RECENT HORSE RIDE ME
    (meaning in the recent past)
FINISH HORSE RIDE ME (meaning "I have ridden the horse.")

**LONG AGO**

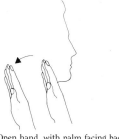

Open hand, with palm facing back, moves past shoulder.

**RECENT**

Hand in "x" position moves down near side of cheek.

**FINISH**

Both hands, palms facing up, rotate until palms face down.

I will go horseback riding.

TOMORROW HORSE RIDE ME
FUTURE HORSE RIDE ME
LATER HORSE RIDE ME

**TOMORROW**

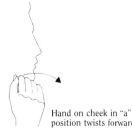

Hand on cheek in "a" position twists forward.

**FUTURE**

Right hand, palm open and facing left, moves forward from side of right cheek.

**LATER**

Right hand in "1" position touches left palm and twists forward.

Tense is indicated only once in the course of an entire message. If the tense changes, the signer introduces a new time word. A fluent signer is able to express as many different aspects of time as a person fluent in English.

## FINGERSPELLED
## LOAN SIGNS

Languages borrow words from other languages. For example, the English colonists did not at first have words for "potato," "squash," or "pumpkin" because they did not have these items in the Old World. They borrowed these words from the American Indians and added them to the English language. "Fry" came from French, "skirt" from Old Norse. The list goes on and on. When cultures mix, their languages influence each other. The culture that has the most political and economic influence will usually contribute more words than it adopts.

Between 1066 and 1700 English borrowed a great many words from French, Latin, and Greek. These languages and the cultures they represented were extremely influential in the Western world. "Government," "crown," "prince," "state," "flower," and "poet" are all French words. "Animal," "poor," "anniversary," and "April" are Latin words. "Drama," "comedy," and "physics" are Greek words. Many other English words have French, Latin, and Greek origins.

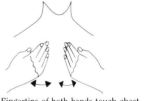

ANIMAL

Fingertips of both hands touch chest
and move toward each other, then away.

Following World War II, the United States became a world power. Nations began borrowing English words and adding them to their everyday vocabulary. The English words "radio" and "jeans," for example, are now part of many different languages, although the accent and pronunciation may vary.

ASL, like other languages, borrows words and signs from other visual languages and then changes them to meet its own needs. French sign had a great influence on ASL due to the efforts of the Frenchman Laurent Clerc, who was a teacher of the deaf in the first permanent school for the deaf in the United States. Today, English has more influence on ASL than French or any other language.

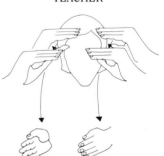

TEACHER

With fingers touching,
move hands from forehead
down and straighten fingers.

When a borrowed word enters ASL, it usually begins with fingerspelling. In fingerspelling the signer uses the fingers of the dominant hand (right hand if you are right-handed, left hand if you are left-handed) to represent each letter in the word being signed. There is a different handshape for each letter in the alphabet. A word is fingerspelled when there is no available sign for it.

The word "job" entered ASL as a fingerspelled word. Originally, it had several different meanings. As time passed, sign-

ers dropped the middle letter, changed the movement, and narrowed the meaning. Ultimately, the fingerspelled configuration evolved into the sign J-B, and it now refers only to employment.

## DIRECTIONALITY

Another feature of ASL is called *directionality*. The direction in which a sign moves can show the relationship between the subject and the object in sentences. Verbs signed in a certain direction can show the patterns of *I to you, you to me, I to it, it to me,* and so on.

GIVE ME

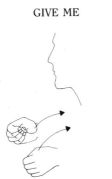

With fingers closed, move
hands toward signer.

GIVE YOU

With fingers closed, moved hands away
from signer and then open them.

When using such verbs as "give," "show," and "look at," it is important to begin the motion of the sign near the message-giver and end the motion near the message-receiver. Did you look at me or did he look at her? These relationships are important. ASL is able to express them through directionality.

## CLASSIFIERS

A unique feature of ASL is the concept of *classifiers*. There is nothing quite like it in English. Classifiers are handshapes that help a signer visually communicate actions and appearances. In English the speaker *talks* about actions, but in ASL the signer *shows* actions. In English the speaker *says* something is round or flat, but in ASL the signer *shows* just how big or small the round or flat object is.

There are two basic groups of classifiers. One group shows the action of nouns. The other shows the size and shape of nouns. There are numerous classifiers within each group. Each classifier has its own handshape and its own special use. The shapes and uses of classifiers continue to evolve as the language changes.

Let's look at noun classifiers first. One noun classifier is used with BOAT, TRAIN, CAR, BICYCLE, and MOTORCYCLE, all forms of transport. The signer uses a single handshape to describe the action of any of these vehicles. For example, in order to describe an automobile trip, the signer first establishes what the classifier will represent (that is, makes the sign for the noun CAR), then uses the classifier to indicate the motion of the car. The sign for CAR need not be used again. By moving the classifier through space, the signer can show that the road is bumpy, slippery, winding, smooth, and so on. The movement can also show the direction and speed of the car. It would be difficult to communicate all this without using classifiers. Classifiers make signing easier.

Let's look at another example. The sign for HORSE is made at the side of the forehead. If a signer wants to talk about several horses playing in the field, he or she would use the classifier. Using the classifier enables the signer to show the various actions of different horses without continually returning the hand to the forehead.

LARGE

A classifier for something large, like a house or a stable.

LARGE FLAT ROUND

The second group of classifiers identifies and describes nouns. FAT, SKINNY, BIG, LARGE, BRUISED ALL OVER, and CANDY BAR can each be represented by a different classifier. For example, when the fingerspelled letter *F* is moved around in different locations, it becomes a classifier and represents flat, round objects such as coins, buttons, and watches. There are many classifiers that begin with a letter in the manual alphabet. For example, if the *L* is made on both the right and left hands, it can indicate flat, round objects such as pancakes or small dishes. If the signer appropriately moves the handshape of the fingerspelled *C*, it can indicate the shape of a cup, a glass, or a can. The context of the sentence and the addition of nonmanual markers make the meaning clear. They are the same facial features described earlier in this chapter:

FLAT ROUND BUTTON

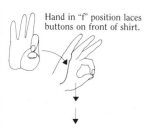

Hand in "f" position laces buttons on front of shirt.

CUP (GLASS)

Right hand in "c" position rests in palm of left hand.

1. Pressed out lips, as if to blow down on your own chin. This means thin.
2. Open mouth, as if to say the word "cha." This means huge, big, large.
3. Pursed lips, as if to whistle. This means small, narrow, smooth.

42

# LET'S PRACTICE

Look at each classifier in column A. Then, from the list below, pick the exact meaning of the sign in column B. The correct answers are on page 44.

a. a parachute
b. a tree trunk
c. someone jumping
d. the number three
e. two people meeting

f. a parking lot
g. two pencils
h. someone drinking
i. buttons
j. someone falling

Column A
*Classifiers*

Column B
*Classifier in Use*

1. any person

Index finger held upright.

2. small round object

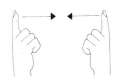

Hand in "f" position laces buttons on front of shirt.

3. vehicle

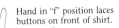

4. shape of a cup, glass, can

5. a person
   (note his two legs)

6. a person

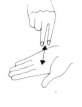

7. something large
   and round

 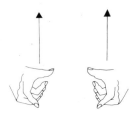

## UNDERSTANDING
## ASL STRUCTURE

Although the English language has been the subject of serious scholarship for many generations, linguists did not begin to examine American Sign Language until quite recently. The first significant study of the structure and nature of ASL began with the work of William Stokoe at Gallaudet College in 1960. Today, linguists continue to study ASL in order to better understand both the people who use the language and the language itself.

*Answers:*

1. e. —two people meeting
2. i. —buttons
3. f. —a parking lot
4. h. —someone drinking
5. c. —someone jumping
6. j. —someone falling
7. b. —a tree trunk

*William Hurt played a teacher of the deaf in the movie* Children of a Lesser God.

To become fluent in any language takes a great deal of practice and exposure to native speakers. There are now more opportunities to learn ASL than ever before. Unlike years ago, when hearing-impaired people were ashamed to "talk" with their hands and bodies in front of hearing people, members of the signing deaf community now take pride in their language and are eager to have others learn it.

ASL is a special form of communication. It has both strong manual and nonmanual components. The manual component is based on the movement, position, palm orientation, and handshapes within a visual space. The nonmanual part relies on the rest of the body. As with other languages, ASL has its own way of doing things. Word order, sentence structure, special ways of using what in English are called pronouns and adjectives, methods of negation, and use of repetition, among other things, are guided by ASL grammar rules. ASL, as you now know, is not signed English but a language in itself. Scholarly information about its unique features continues to be gathered.

MORE

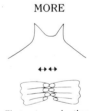

Fingers tap each other.

45

# 4
# Silent Speech

FLOOR

HAPPEN

With palms up, fingers closed
except for index finger, turn
hands over so palms face down.

Starting a conversation in sign language is different from starting a conversation in a spoken language. In a spoken language it's possible to begin a conversation with a person who is reading a book or even in another room. It's even common, although not always polite, to enter a conversation by interrupting with a word or a cough. None of these things can be done in a visual language.

In order to start a conversation in sign language it is necessary to get a person's visual attention. There are various ways to do this. Tapping the shoulder or touching the person's arm are two common attention getters. Another way is to stamp a foot. As long as the floor is not carpeted or made of a sound-absorbent material, a deaf person is likely to feel the vibration and respond to it. After getting the person's attention, a signer may begin a conversation by trying to arouse the other person's curiosity. This could be done by dramatically signing a descriptive word such as THRILL, AWFUL, or HAPPEN. The hope is that the expression on the face, the body movements, and the sign itself will make the receiver want to find out what is *thrilling, awful,* or *what's happening.* If this happens the person will look directly at the signer for more information. Thus, a conversation begins.

46

*Students at a Model Secondary School for the
Deaf learn science the way hearing students do, by
experimenting and asking questions.*

In order to interrupt the speaker and still show good manners, the one who desires to cut in makes a sudden movement into the sign space, such as waving an outstretched hand. The sign space, as indicated before, is the area in front of and to both sides of the signer. It is the area used to make the signs.

The following pages contain several dialogs that can help you get started communicating in sign language. Some of the signs should already be familiar to you because they were used as examples in the previous chapter.

| Dialogue | Sign Explanations |
|---|---|

(Words to be signed are capitalized. Words in lower case are not signed. Words to be fingerspelled are hyphenated. Numbers indicate ASL word order.)

1. Jessica: HELLO, may I SIT down?

Tilt head and move eyebrows up for question.

HELLO

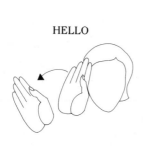

I

SIT

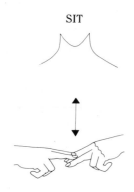

2. Marcy: SURE. BRING over a CHAIR.

CHAIR is signed before BRING because CHAIR is the topic.

SURE

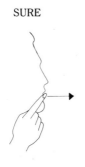

CHAIR

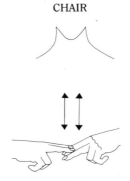

BRING

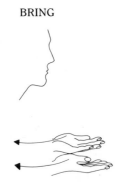

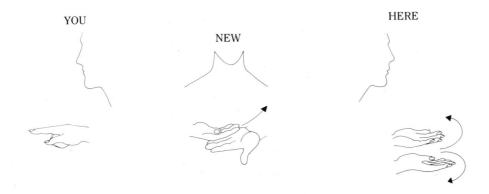

4  5  6
Are YOU NEW HERE?          Eyebrows move up for
                          question form.

YOU                                                    HERE

NEW

3. Jessica:  1   3   2                NAME is signed before
             YES. MY NAME is          the pronoun MY, and
             4       5                FRIENDS is signed be-
             JESSICA BROWN. We

YES                        NAME                    MY

Right hand moves back and forth      Two fingers of right hand tap
against side of lower body.          two fingers of left hand.

                                      BROWN

JESSICA

The name sign for Jessica            Sign for the color brown.
is "j" shape.

49

<sup>6</sup>       <sup>7</sup>
MOVED here FROM

<sup>8</sup>       <sup>12</sup>
K-A-N-S-A-S, and I

<sup>10</sup>   <sup>9</sup>
have NO FRIENDS

<sup>11</sup>
YET.

fore the word NO. (In ASL the words that describe the noun usually follow the noun.) In this dialogue the ASL sign for NO is NONE or ZERO. Both name signs and fingerspelling are used in ASL. Name signs are made-up signs, usually beginning with the fingerspelled first letter of the person's name. Sometimes the name sign describes the person. The names of states are usually fingerspelled.

MOVED

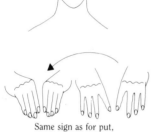

Same sign as for put, moving to the side.

FROM

(fingerspell KANSAS)

FRIENDS

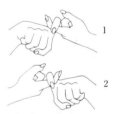

1

2

Index fingers lock.
Hands switch position and repeat motion.

NO

YET

I

50

4. Marcy: 
$\overset{2}{\text{MY}}$ $\overset{1}{\text{NAME}}$ IS $\overset{3}{\text{MARCY}}$
$\overset{4}{\text{WHITE.}}$ $\overset{5}{\text{I}}$ $\overset{6}{\text{HOPE}}$ $\overset{7}{\text{YOU}}$
$\overset{8}{\text{LIKE}}$ it $\overset{9}{\text{HERE.}}$

Nod the head to indicate a positive statement.

**NAME**

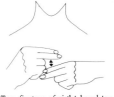

Two fingers of right hand tap two fingers of left hand.

**MY**

**MARCY**

Hand in "m" position, made on cheek, moves down.

**WHITE**

Right fingers touch chest, then move away with fingers closing over thumbs.

**I**

**HOPE**

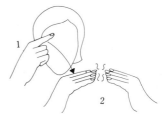

Right index finger touches forehead and moves down. Fingers on both hands move as if waving.

**YOU**

**LIKE**

Thumb and middle finger touch, then pull out from chest, closing over thumb.

**HERE**

51

5. Jessica:   THANKS, I HOPE SO TOO.

$\overset{1}{\phantom{x}}\overset{2}{\phantom{x}}\overset{3}{\phantom{x}}\overset{4}{\phantom{x}}$

What do YOU D-O for    *Do* is fingerspelled.

FUN?

THANKS

I

HOPE

Right index finger touches forehead and moves down.
Fingers on both hands move as if waving.

TOO

Index fingers move together.

YOU

FUN

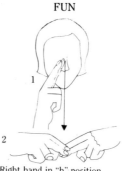

(fingerspell DO)

Right hand in "h" position
touches side of nose. Hand moves
down to rest on left hand.

52

6. Marcy: 
     <sup>1</sup> OH, the usual.

     <sup>2</sup> MOVIES, <sup>3</sup> DANCING,

     <sup>4</sup> GOLF, <sup>5</sup> BOWLING,

     <sup>6</sup> FOOTBALL games

     in the <sup>7</sup> FALL,

     <sup>8</sup> BASKETBALL in

     the <sup>9</sup> WINTER,

When showing the various sports, pantomime the movements of those sports.

**OH**

Hand in "y" position moves up and down.

**MOVIES**

Hand closest to body moves back and forth.

**DANCING**

Two fingers swing across open palm.

**GOLF**

Clasp hands as if holding a golfclub.

**BOWLING**

Use natural gesture as if bowling.

**FOOTBALL**

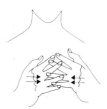

Fingers move in and out.

**FALL**

Right hand brushes lower left arm near elbow twice.

**BASKETBALL**

Both hands throw imaginary basketball over head.

**WINTER**

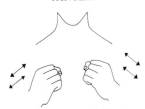

Shake both fists as if shivering.

53

10
SWIMMING whenever the pool's free,

11 12 13
SOMETIMES TEACHING HEARING

14 15
PEOPLE SIGN language.

SOMETIMES

SWIMMING

Hands make natural gesture of swimming
the breast stroke.

Right index finger strikes left palm twice,
as if striking a match.

HEARING

TEACHING

Index finger moves out from mouth,
in corkscrew motion.

SIGN

PEOPLE

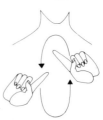

Hold both hands in "p" position and
make alternate circles.

Index fingers are up,
with palms out. Hands move
in alternate circles.

7. Jessica: Do MANY[1] PEOPLE[2] RIDE[3]?

Eyebrows up for question form. There are several signs for RIDE, but the one to use here indicates the visual image of a straddle.

MANY

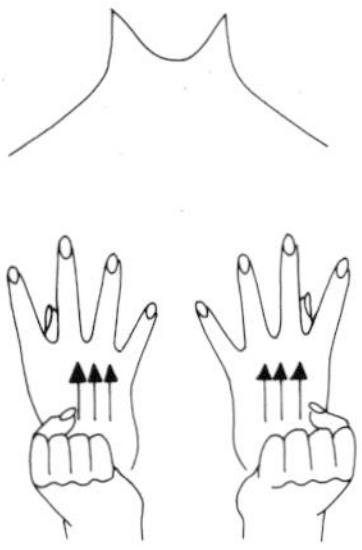

Fingers spring up quickly. Repeat motion.

PEOPLE

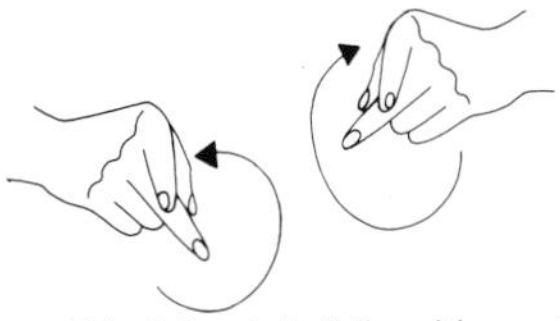

Hold both hands in "p" position and make alternate circles.

RIDE

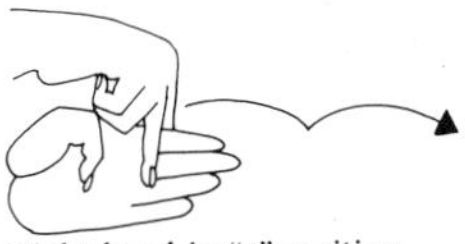

Right hand in "v" position straddles left forefinger. Both hands move forward.

8. Marcy: RIDE?[1] RIDE[2] WHAT?[3] CARS,[4] BIKES,[5] MOTORCYCLES?[6]

Eyebrows up for question form.

RIDE

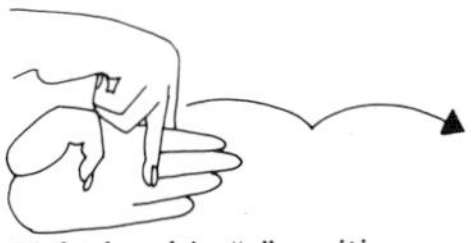

Right hand in "v" position straddles left forefinger. Both hands move forward.

RIDE

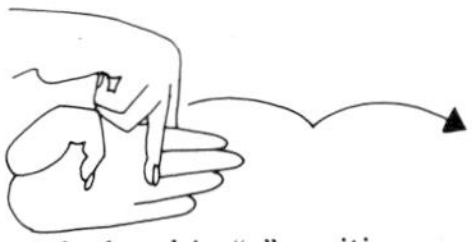

Right hand in "v" position straddles left forefinger. Both hands move forward.

WHAT

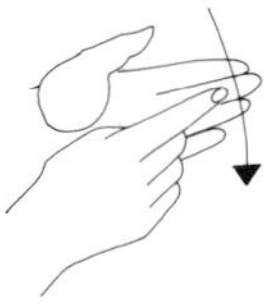

Index finger of right hand moves down across fingers of left hand.

CARS

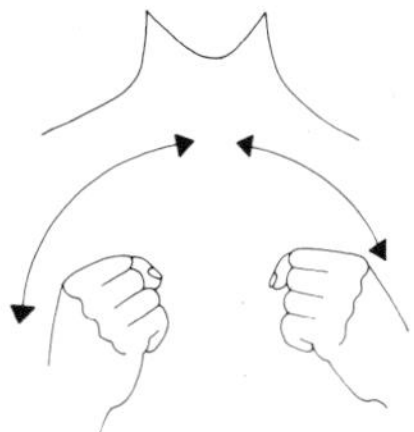

Hands hold imaginary steering wheel and pretend to drive.

BIKES

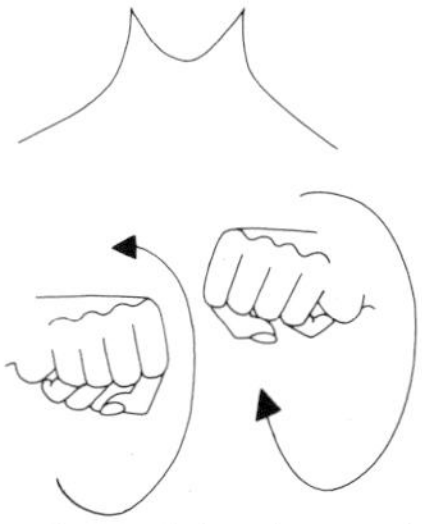

Two fists push imaginary pedals in alternating circles.

MOTORCYCLES

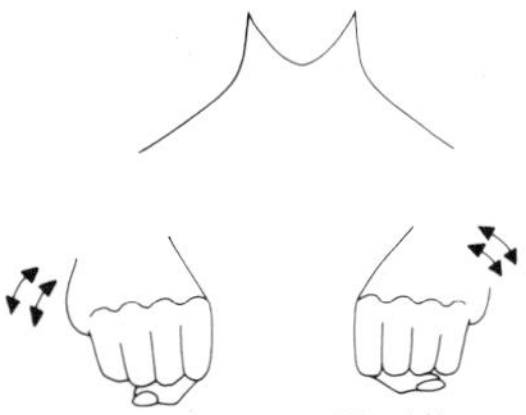

Fists twists as if holding motorcycle handles.

9. Jessica:    ¹ ²
               HORSES! Do YOU
               ³      ⁴
               RIDE HORSES?

Emphasis on the first
sign HORSES. Eyebrows
up for question form
in the second part of
the sentence.

HORSES

With thumb touching temple
and two fingers together,
hand moves up and down.

YOU

HORSES

With thumb touching temple
and two fingers together,
hand moves up and down.

RIDE

Right hand in "v" position
straddles left forefinger.
Both hands move forward.

10. Marcy:    ¹
              YES. I've been
                ²
              RIDING for many

Instead of signing
MANY, repeat YEARS sev-
eral times to show

YES

Right hand moves back and forth
against side of lower body.

RIDING

Right hand in "v" position
straddles left forefinger.
Both hands move forward.

56

                    3       4      7
                YEARS, BUT I HAVE
                    5      6
                NO HORSE of my

                own.

that the activity hap-
pened many times.
HORSE is signed before
NO and HAVE because it
is the next topic in
this sentence.

### YEARS

Closed right hand circles around left fist.
Repeat several times.

### BUT

Index fingers cross, then move apart,
palms down.

### NO

Hands with fingers in "o" position
move away from each other.

### HORSES

With thumb touching temple
and two fingers together,
hand moves up and down.

### HAVE

Tips of both hands touch upper chest.

8
On SATURDAY

9
AFTERNOONS a

10   11  12
FRIEND AND I

13
CARPOOL to a

15
STABLE out in the

14
COUNTRY.

CARPOOL is signed as a combination of two signs: GET-IN (a vehicle) and RIDE. COUNTRY is signed before STABLE because COUNTRY describes where the stable is located. A classifier is used to replace STABLE the second time it is used.

AFTERNOONS

FRIEND

1

2

Index fingers lock.
Hands switch position
and repeat motion.

SATURDAY

Hand in "s" position circles
clockwise in air.

AND

I

CARPOOL

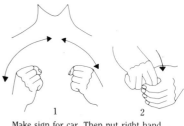

1               2

Make sign for car. Then put right hand,
with bent index and middle finger
in "c" position in left hand.

With right hand, palm facing in,
fingers come together
as hand moves to right.

COUNTRY

Right hand touches and circles
lower arm near left elbow.

STABLE

(see classifier for large)
Right "claw" hand
indicates building placement.

16   17     18          19
WE TAKE  LESSONS. MAYBE

 20        21      22
YOU can TAKE  LESSONS, too.


TAKE

LESSONS

WE

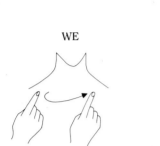

Right index finger touches upper right chest,
then upper left chest.

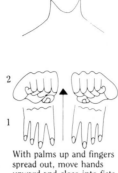

With palms up and fingers
spread out, move hands
upward and close into fists.

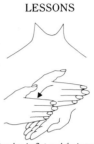

Left palm is flat and facing up,
while right hand rests
at a right angle on top.
Right hand moves down.


MAYBE            YOU            TAKE

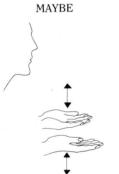

Palms face up. Both hands move
up and down alternately.

With palms up and fingers
spread out, move hands
upward and close into fists.

LESSONS

Left palm is flat and facing up,
while right hand rests
at a right angle on top.
Right hand moves down.

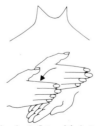

59

11. Jessica:  It SOUNDS¹ LIKE²
             FUN.³ I-F⁴ the STABLE⁵
             is NOT⁶ too FAR-AWAY,⁷
             MAYBE⁸ MY¹⁰ MOTHER⁹
             will DRIVE¹¹ me.

Sounds do not mean anything to a deaf person, so the sign for SEEMS is used here. LIKE is signed as SAME. When signing NOT, shake your head to make it negative.

**SOUNDS**

Right cupped palm turns slightly inward toward face.

**LIKE**

Thumb and middle finger touch, then pull out from chest, closing over thumb.

**FUN**

Right hand in "h" position touches side of nose. Hand moves down to rest on left hand.

(fingerspell IF)

**STABLE**

(see classifier for large)
Right "claw" hand indicates building placement.

## NOT

## FAR AWAY

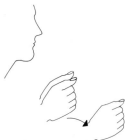

Hands start out together.
Right hand move ahead.

## MAYBE

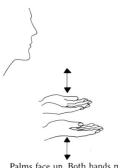

Palms face up. Both hands move
up and down alternately.

## MOTHER

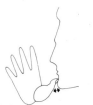

Thumb touches chin.

## MY

## DRIVE

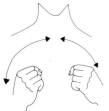

Hands are in "s" position
as if steering a car.

12. Marcy:  MY FATHER is DRIVING THIS-WEEK. MY GRANDfather drives NEXT-WEEK. I-F you JOIN us, someone in YOUR FAMILY CAN DRIVE in TWO-WEEKS.

THIS-WEEK AND NEXT-WEEK are signed before DRIVE. In ASL, time and place are usually established first. After I-F (you) JOIN (us), shift your body slightly to show that this is a conditional sentence and therefore has two parts. CAN is signed last, to give emphasis to the conditional part of the sentence.

THIS WEEK

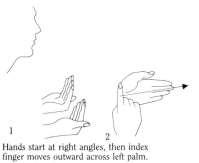

Hands start at right angles, then index finger moves outward across left palm.

FATHER

Right thumb touches forehead, then fingers wiggle.

MY

DRIVING

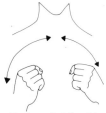

Hands are in "s" position as if steering a car.

62

### NEXT WEEK

Right index finger moves
across left palm and up.

### GRANDFATHER

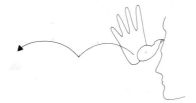

### MY

### JOIN

### DRIVES

(fingerspell IF)

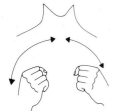

Hands are in "s" position
as if steering a car.

Right index and middle finger
move into left hand, which is
in the "c" position.

### TWO WEEKS

### FAMILY

Both hands in "f" position
make circle moving downward
in front of body.

### YOUR

### DRIVE

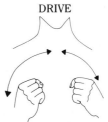

Hands are in "s" position
as if steering a car.

### CAN

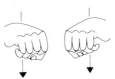

13. Jessica:  <sup>1</sup>SOUNDS <sup>2</sup>GOOD to me.

Fingerspell SCUBA DIVE. Eyebrows up for question.

<sup>3</sup>Does ANYONE around

<sup>4</sup>here KNOW how to

<sup>5</sup>S-C-U-B-A D-I-V-E?

SOUNDS

Right cupped palm turns slightly inward toward face.

GOOD

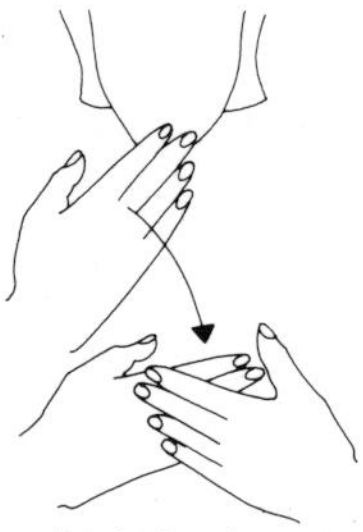

Closed right hand goes into "c" position on left side.

ANYONE

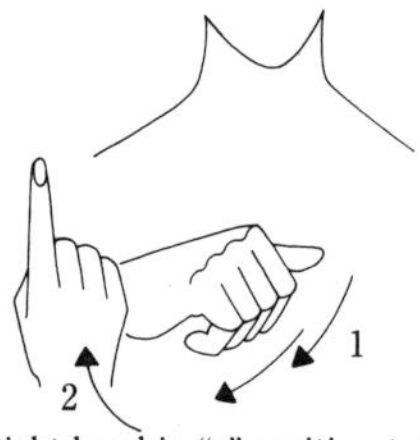

Right hand in "a" position twists to the side. Then index finger points up.

KNOW

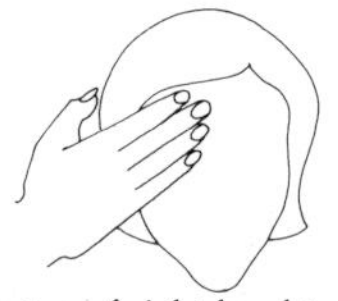

Fingers of right hand tap upper right corner of forehead.

(fingerspell SCUBA DIVE)

14. Marcy:  <sup>1</sup> <sup>2</sup> <sup>3</sup>
NO-ONE SWIMS IN

<sup>4</sup>
the LAKE. The

<sup>5</sup>
WATER is too

<sup>6</sup>
POLLUTED.

**NO ONE**

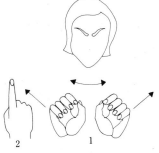

Both hands in "o" position move
at an angle away from the body.
Right hand ends with index finger up,
palm facing in.
Head moves side to side also.

**SWIMS**

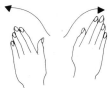

Hands make natural gesture of swimming
the breast stroke.

**IN**

Open hand, with palm facing back,
moves past shoulder.

**LAKE**

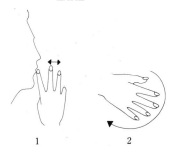

Hand in "w" position touches lips. Then open hand,
with palm down, makes a half-circle,
indicating space.

**WATER**

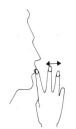

With right hand in "w" position,
index finger taps mouth.

**POLLUTED**

Top of hand touches chin
while fingers wiggle.

65

Our
10  9
SCIENCE CLASS had
8
a project LAST
7
SPRING. We
11
CLEANED-UP the
12
WATER. It was an
14  13
ENORMOUS JOB. Do
15  16
you KNOW WHAT we
17  18  19
FOUND IN the WATER?

LAST SPRING is signed before SCIENCE CLASS. ASL places time and place first. Be sure to use lots of facial expressions to emphasize the sign ENORMOUS. It is more than just big. Eyebrows go up for question.

SPRING

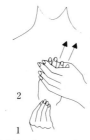

Right hand opens as it pushes up through left hand in "c" position. Repeat motion.

LAST

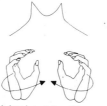

With open palm facing in, fingers touch mouth and move out into left palm.

CLASS

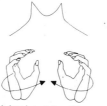

Both hands in "c" position move as if to shape a ball.

SCIENCE

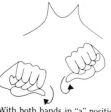

With both hands in "a" position, thumbs point down and make small circles.

66

## CLEANED UP

Open right hand moves quickly back and
forth across left palm.

## WATER

With right hand in "w" position,
index finger taps mouth.

## JOB

Right fist hits top of left fist
in knocking motion.

## ENORMOUS

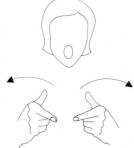

Hands in bent "1" position move away
from each other, indicating large size.
Mouth is open in "cha" shape.

## KNOW

Fingers of right hand tap upper
right corner of forehead.

## WHAT

Index finger of right
hand moves down
across fingers of left hand.

## FOUND

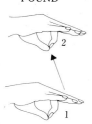

## IN

Open hand, with palm facing back,
moves past shoulder.

## WATER

With right hand in "w" position,
index finger taps mouth.

15. Jessica:    ¹WHAT?

Sign this with dramatic movement and facial expression.

WHAT

Index finger of right
hand moves down
across fingers of left hand.

16. Marcy:    A ²NO ³S-K-A-T-I-N-G
             ¹SIGN.

Fingerspell SKATING. The Skating sign is indicated by drawing its shape in space. Note that the word "sign" here is different from the word *sign* in *sign language*.

SIGN

With index fingers up, palms out,
move hands in alternate circles.

NO

Hands with fingers in "o" position
move away from each other.

(fingerspell SKATING)

Using the next two hand dialogs, see if you can have a sign language conversation with a friend. As usual, the words to be signed are printed in capital letters. However, illustrations are given only for those signs not previously shown in this book.

## ASL Dialog 2

Todd:  HI.
Geoff:  HI.
Todd:  You LOOK AWFUL. Are you SICK?

LOOK

Right index finger moves
counterclockwise around the face.

TERRIBLE (AWFUL)

Finger and thumb flick outward.

SICK

Geoff:  It's been a TERRIBLE DAY. I started out FEELING BLUE,

DAY

FEELING

Middle finger touches signer's
chest and moves up.

BLUE (SAD)

69

BECAUSE MY BEST FRIEND is MOVING. I RODE MY BIKE to

### BECAUSE

Index finger moves across forehead,
ending in an "a" position.

### BEST

Hand moves across mouth and
ends in an "a" position.

HIS HOUSE, and I FELL OFF. NOW I'm BRUISED ALL OVER

### HIS

### HOUSE

### FELL OFF

Right hand, in "v" position, stands on
palm of left hand and falls off.

AND my STOMACH HURTS, too.

### STOMACH

### HURTS

Index fingers move in and out.

Todd: FROM WHAT? FALLING OFF YOUR BICYCLE?
Geoff: NO, I FEEL FAT. I ATE TOO MUCH for LUNCH.

LUNCH

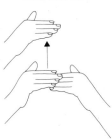

ATE

Use natural gesture for eating.

TOO MUCH

The sign for eat ends with two
fingers flicking up.

Todd: WHAT did you EAT?
Geoff: HOT-DOGS AND a tossed SALAD.

SALAD

Move as though tossing lettuce.

Todd: SOUNDS perfectly GOOD to me. WHY are you SICK?

WHY

Fingers touch forehead and move outward,
ending in "y" position.

71

Geoff: But I ATE FIVE HOT-DOGS!
Todd: ANYTHING MORE?

FIVE

ANY

With hand in "a" position, palm in,
twist so that palm faces out.

MORE

Geoff: YES. I WAS THIRSTY, SO I DRANK a STRAWBERRY ICE CREAM
S-O-D-A.

THIRSTY

Index finger touches throat,
then moves down.

DRANK

Natural gesture, as if
drinking from a glass.

STRAWBERRY

Right hand grasps left small finger and
twists it back and forth.

ICE CREAM

Hand in "s" position moves down across
lips several times.

**Todd:** THAT'S WHY YOU FEEL SO AWFUL. YOU BETTER GO HOME.

THAT'S

BETTER

Right hand, palm in, moves
across mouth and then in slight upward
motion ends in "a" position.

GO

Movement is out and away from signer.

HOME

Fingers together touch mouth,
then side of cheek.

# ASL Dialog 3

**Jill:** TOMORROW is MY BIRTHDAY. CAN you COME?

BIRTHDAY

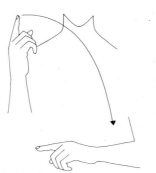

Both hands, palms in, move away from body.
Then the sign for day is made.

COME

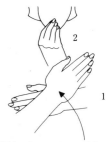

This is the opposite movement of go.

**Ruth:** What TIME?

**Jill:** EARLY. We START with a BREAKFAST picnic at the z-o-o and END with a SLEEPOVER.

EARLY

Finger moves down across left hand.

START

Right index finger twists
between middle and
index finger of left hand.

BREAKFAST

Right hand moves up at right
angles to left horizontal arm.
Then the sign for eat is made.

END

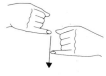

SLEEPOVER

Open right hand moves down face as
fingers close. Right hand then moves over left
arm at right angles and twists.

Ruth:   IN TENTS at the z-o-o? Sounds GREAT!

GREAT

TENTS

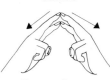

Fingers pull apart.

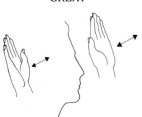

Hands move rapidly forward and back.

Jill:   NO, IN BEDS at the Sleepyhollow MOTEL. We just SEE the
ANIMALS at the z-o-o, NOT SLEEP NEAR ANIMALS.

BEDS

NEAR

MOTEL

Hand in "m" shape twists
back and forth.

Open right hand hits back of left hand.

Ruth:   What HAPPENS if it RAINS?

RAINS

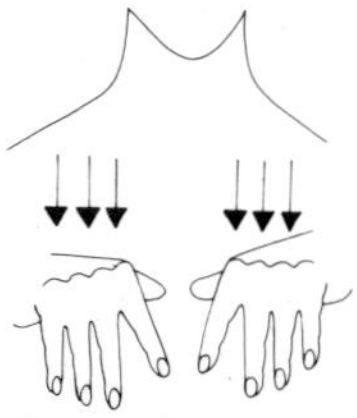

Hands move down repeatedly.


Jill:   WE get WET.

WET

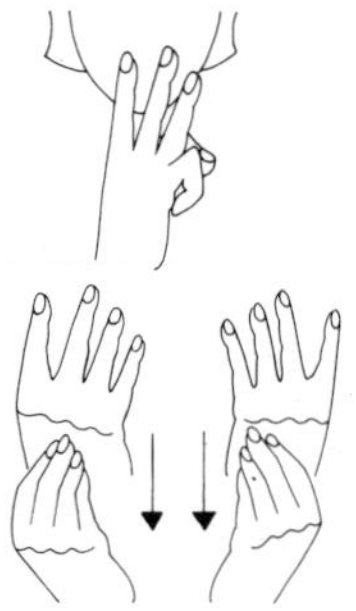

Hand in "w" position touches mouth,
then both hands move away from
the body with fingers closing.


Ruth:   What HAPPENS if it really RAINS-HARD?

RAINS HARD

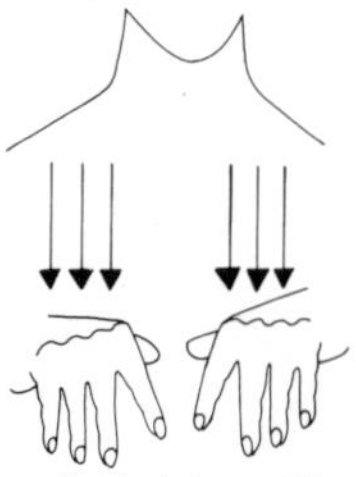

Same as rains but done with more force.

Jill:    WE get WET.

Ruth:   MAYBE I'LL BRING an UMBRELLA.

Jill:    SUIT-YOURSELF. AFTER the Z-O-O we have LUNCH at MY HOUSE.

SUIT YOURSELF

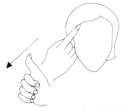

Index finger touches forehead, then moves away,
ending in "a" position.

Ruth:   WHAT'S for LUNCH?

Jill:    HOT-DOGS.

Ruth:   What HAPPENS if I DON'T LIKE HOT-DOGS?

DON'T LIKE

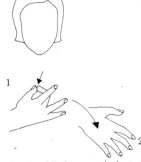

Thumb and middle finger touch chest, then move away,
with fingers opening and palm twisting to face floor.

Jill:    You CAN EAT a SANDWICH.

SANDWICH

Both hands are brought, palms together,
toward mouth.

Ruth:   I LIKE HOT-DOGS.
Jill:    GOOD. THEN we SEE MOVIES AND PLAY GAMES.

PLAY

THEN

Right hand, palm in, moves up
and over left hand, palm also in.

Both hands in "y" position shake.

GAMES

Both hands in "a" position
move together.

Ruth:   WILL we have POPCORN?

WILL

Right hand, palm facing left, moves out from
side of right cheek.

POPCORN

Index fingers on both hands flick up alternately.

78

Jill:    OF-COURSE! CAN'T SEE A MOVIE WITHOUT POPCORN!

OF COURSE

Right hand in "n" position circles above left fist
and then rests on top.

CAN'T

Right index finger moves down, brushing
top of left index finger.

Ruth:    I HATE POPCORN.

HATE

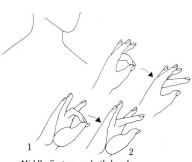

1                    2

Middle fingers on both hands
flick straight out.

Jill:    NATURALLY! BUT you CAN WATCH the MOVIE WITHOUT POP-
CORN.

WATCH

79

Ruth:  Will I LIKE the MOVIE?
Jill:  I DON'T-KNOW. BUT if you don't you CAN PLAY GAMES.
Ruth:  NAME the GAMES.
Jill:  PING-PONG, POOL, V-I-D-E-O GAMES. AFTER the MOVIE we GO SWIMMING.

PING PONG

Natural gesture, as if hitting a ping pong ball, is made.

POOL

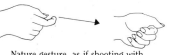

Nature gesture, as if shooting with a cue stick, is made.

AFTER

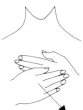

Right hand touches back of left hand, then moves away.

Ruth:  Do you have your OWN POOL?
Jill:  NO. We WILL have to DRIVE to the MOTEL for that. It's a WONDERFUL PLACE. It even HAS a DIVING BOARD.

OWN POOL

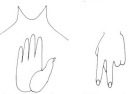

With palm out, fingerspell the word pool. Begin with "p." P-O-O-L.

DIVING BOARD

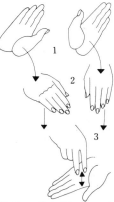

PLACE

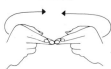

With both hands in "p" position, middle fingers touch and make a circle, palms down, in front of signer.

Starting with both arms overhead, hands are moved down in diving motion. Then index and middle finger jump up and down on opposite palm.

**Ruth:** I CAN'T SWIM.

**Jill:** W-E-L-L, you CAN HELP COOK the barbecue (B-B-Q) for
dinner.

COOK

HELP

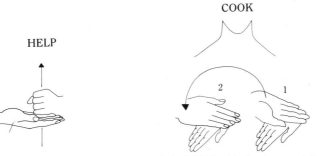

Back of right hand is placed on open left palm,
then slips over it.

**Ruth:** WHAT NEXT?

**Jill:** MORE GAMES, THEN STORY-TELLING by a storyteller, and
FINALLY S-N-A-C-K-S AND a SLUMBER PARTY. WILL YOU COME?

PARTY

STORYTELLING

FINALLY

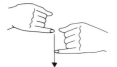

Thumb and forefinger of each hand interlock,
then pull away and close. Repeat motion.

Right little finger move down, hitting top
of left little finger.

With hands in "p" position,
make circles in the air.

**Ruth:** YES! I CAN'T WAIT!

WAIT

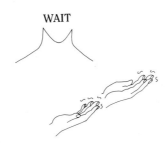

# 5
## Games

GOOD

Facial expressions, body movement, and sign formation are essential to American Sign Language. The more animated and dramatic a signer is, the easier it is for others to understand the communication. It takes visual imagination, and an ability to use the body, to be a really good signer. Not every deaf person is a good signer. Nor is every hearing person a good speaker.

Except for actors, few English-speaking people deliberately use their bodies to communicate. Although most people tend to make occasional gestures when they speak, pointing is considered rude, and excessive movement is frowned upon. Parents and teachers of hearing children teach them to hold still and not "talk with their hands." Thus, when hearing people begin to learn ASL, they often find it difficult to make correct hand gestures and to properly use facial expressions. Most English-speaking people are self-conscious about using their bodies to communicate.

Exercises and practice can help people become less self-conscious, relax their bodies, and loosen facial muscles. Games can do the same thing. Here are a few fun games requiring partners that will encourage you to use your whole body to communicate and should stimulate your imagination. Stand

82

in groups of two, facing each other. There is no limit to the number of pairs that may play at one time.

## "FUNNY FACE"

In "Funny Face," partner A and partner B must look at each other but may not touch each other. Partner A makes funny faces and body movements in an attempt to make partner B laugh. The job of partner B is to look sad in as many different ways as possible. The winner is the first one who can get the other one to change facial expressions: from happy to sad or sad to happy. Reverse roles and play again. Think of new emotions and repeat the challenge.

TOUCH

## "MIRROR MIRROR"

In this game, partner A pretends to be a full-length mirror. Partner B peers into the mirror and moves face, hands, and body in any way desired. Partner A must copy exactly what partner B is doing while partner B is doing it. The partners may not touch each other. Reverse roles and play again.

## "PUPPET PULL"

In "Puppet Pull," partner A pretends to be a marionette. Partner B operates the strings. Reverse roles and play again.

## "MAKE A MODEL"

STRING

Partner A is a sculptor and partner B is a lump of clay. Partner A forms partner B into the shape of something or someone by arranging his or her partner's hands, feet, head, lips, and so on.

## "PRETEND TO BE"

This game does not require partners. You just pretend to be:

a. a hot dog on a bun who likes relish, sauerkraut, and mustard but hates ketchup and pickles
b. a pen out of ink or a pencil with a broken point
c. a cockroach and a can of insect destroyer
d. a kettle of boiling water

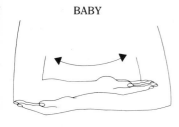
BABY

e. an old man or an old woman
f. a baby learning to walk
g. a sleepwalker
h. a spider spinning a web
i. a fish, animal, or plant of your choice (with or without a partner)
j. anything you want.

## "CIRCLE LEFT"

By yourself or in a large circle with all participants facing left, move as though you were walking through:

a. mud
b. gum
c. fire
d. water
e. hot sand, barefoot
f. knee-deep snow
g. a field of pebbles, barefoot
h. your favorite food up to your waist.

Now that your body, face, and hands can express a variety of feelings and activities, here are some sign language games that can help you become a better signer and a better sign language receiver. The signs used are all based on things you have learned in this book. As you learn additional signs and more complicated sentence patterns, adapt the games accordingly.

## "HOT DOGS AND HORSES"

The first player makes a statement based on the information in one of the dialogs in this or the preceding chapter. The statement contains a blank that one of the other players must fill in by choosing one of three possibilities given by player one. Only one sign can be correct. For example, player one says: "Geoff ate —————." Player one then signs three words: HOT-DOGS, HORSE, and CAR. If player two signs HOT-DOGS (the only possible correct answer), it is his or her turn to give a sentence. If HORSE or CAR is signed, then player one goes again. Player one continues with new sentences, until player two gets the right answer.

84

## "ODD ONE OUT"

Player one makes four signs. Three signs form a group. One sign does not belong. Player two gives the sign that does not belong. For example, player one gives the signs for MOTHER, BASKETBALL, FATHER, and GRANDMOTHER. Player two signs BASKETBALL, because all the other words are relatives. Relatives form a group.

Use your imagination to define a group. A group could be all signs that have a certain palm orientation, words that all begin with the same letter, or all descriptive words.

## "PICTURE PUZZLE"

Player one signs a simple picture description, such as:

| | |
|---|---|
| horse in lake | black bicycle near stable |
| popcorn for movies | sandwich for lunch |

Player two must translate the signs orally into spoken English. For a fancier version of this game, build the sentences into a story. Each signer adds a picture; each receiver interprets the sign.

## "MATCHMAKER"

This game is best when played with ten or more people. Take ten sheets of paper. On each of five sheets write a different word for which the sign is known. Then, on the other five sheets, draw a picture of the sign for each word. There should be no more than one word or one sign on each sheet. Attach one sheet to the back of each player. The player must not know whether a word or a sign is there. At a given signal and without speaking, players must search for the person who has the translation of the word or sign that is on his or her own back. The first one to find a match wins, but the game is not over until everyone finds a match.

## "TELL ME A STORY"

Each person receives a list of several nouns for which the signs are known. One person begins telling a story. Each time the storyteller comes to a noun, he or she stops, and any player

**FOR**

index touches forehead and twists out.

**BLACK**

Hand in "a" position shakes back and forth.

**TEN**

Hand in "a" position shakes back and forth.

**STORYTELLING**

Thumb and forefinger of each hand interlock, then pull away and close. Repeat motion.

who has a noun that can reasonably fit the story signs it. The first player continues telling the story until all the nouns are used up. Then another storyteller is selected. The game is over when all the nouns have been placed in the story.

## "SIGN RELAY"

Two or more teams play. The teams line up in single file. Each team has a judge. All judges have identical lists of words, but in a different order. At a given signal each judge says the first word to the person at the head of the line. The player will sign the word. If the sign is correct, the judge gives the second word to the next player. If the sign is not correct, the same word is given to the second player. The team that gets through the list of words first wins.

TEAM

Move hands in circle downward in front of body.

## "SIGN LANGUAGE BASEBALL"

Everyone is divided into two teams. Each team has a symbol, such as *S* or *L*. One player draws a diamond on the chalkboard. The leader then gives a member of one team a word to sign. If he or she signs it correctly, the symbol for that team is put on first base. If the word is missed, the player is "struck out." The leader gives the next word to a member of the opposing team. If it is signed correctly, the symbol for that team is put on first base. Players from opposing teams may be on a base at the same time. Succeeding words signed correctly cause the symbol to be advanced one base at a time, until "home plate" is reached. The team obtaining the most runs is the winner.

If no chalkboard is available, the game may be played with paper. In this case a diamond is drawn on the paper and the players advance using colored markers. Each team has a different color.

## "TRANSLATION TROUBLE"

Player A makes a sign and calls on player B, who must say what the sign is. If player B answers correctly, it will be that player's turn to sign and someone else's turn to guess. The game continues until everyone has had a turn.

## "SIGN THE ANSWER"

Here is a sign language version of twenty questions. It will give you practice in forming the signs. Answer the questions by giving the appropriate sign. The answers appear at the end of the list.

OLD

1. What has four legs and a back?
2. What do you call a person you like very much?
3. What do you sign when you meet another person?
4. What is the opposite of old?
5. What do you get when you are born?
6. Name a game that is played with a large, heavy, three-holed ball.
7. What is the sign for more than one person?
8. What has two wheels, two pedals, and handlebars?
9. What comes before night?
10. If you can expect to find tall buildings and subways in the city, where would you find barns and haywagons?
11. What are the signs for male and female parents?
12. What does the person sitting behind the steering wheel of an automobile do?
13. Who is your father's father?
14. What do you call the people you live with?
15. What do people generally do in a swimming pool?
16. What game is played on the grass with clubs and a small white ball?
17. What season comes after winter?
18. What is the opposite of dirty?
19. What is the opposite of bad?
20. Name an animal that lives in a barn and is strong enough to transport people from place to place.

NIGHT

Closed fist touches chin and moves down.

BAD

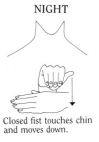

*Answers:*

| | | |
|---|---|---|
| 1. CHAIR | 8. BIKE | 15. SWIM |
| 2. FRIEND | 9. AFTERNOON | 16. GOLF |
| 3. HELLO | 10. COUNTRY | 17. SPRING |
| 4. NEW | 11. MOTHER, FATHER | 18. CLEAN |
| 5. NAME | 12. DRIVE | 19. GOOD |
| 6. BOWLING | 13. GRANDFATHER | 20. HORSE |
| 7. PEOPLE | 14. FAMILY | |

*Actors in the National Theatre of the Deaf create
the sign for "spirit" while performing the play*
The Dybbuk: Between Two Worlds, *a fantasy and
love story set in a world not quite our own.*

# 6

# Poetry and Music

In a spoken language, when a poet or an actor recites a poem, every syllable of every word in that poem must be said loudly and clearly. Nothing must be left out. The sounds of the words as well as the meanings of the words combine to create the rhythm, pattern, and beauty of the poem. Poems, however, are more than words. They are moods, ideas, and emotions. In order to express these things, the speaker needs to interpret the poem through voice by adjusting rate of speech, tone of voice, and emphasis. Reciting a poem is, in effect, like giving a dramatic presentation. To do it well requires thought and imagination.

Signing poetry also requires thought and imagination. However, the process of visually presenting a poem rather than orally presenting it is quite different. In signing poetry, the goal is to express the poet's thoughts and feelings visually in space. The entire visual image is designed to capture the rhythm, pattern, and beauty of the original poem. In order to do this, the signer needs to adjust the tempo, size, and rhythm of the signs. The signer also needs to use facial expressions, nonmanual markers, and body language. It is perfectly acceptable to leave out words that add nothing visual to the poem and also to change the order of words.

MUSIC

Open right hand, palm facing left, moves back and forth in arclike motion.

FEELING

Middle finger touches signer's chest and moves up.

89

PICTURE

Right hand in "c" position is held near eye, then moves into open left palm.

Signing poetry is not easy. However, a person can begin to learn how to do it by working with haiku. Haiku is a form of Japanese poetry that is limited to seventeen syllables in three lines. It tries to create a single picture. In order to sign a haiku poem, the signer first needs to think carefully about the true meaning of the poem. Once the signer is satisfied with an interpretation, he or she then picks out signs and combines them in ASL order to convey the poem's meaning visually. Signing poetry can be as creative as writing it.

A few simple steps will help you get started learning how to sign poetry. First of all, here's a poem you can work with:

### Happy Day

*A rainy Saturday*
*My friend and I at play*
*Make a happy day*

1. *Create a picture of the poem in your mind.* Visualize you and your best friend doing something enjoyable on a rainy Saturday. Be very specific in your choice. Decide exactly where the activity is taking place and what time of day it is. Was it raining hard or just sprinkling? You are creating a mental picture. What you don't see and feel, your audience will not see and feel.

2. *Think about the poet's feelings.* Was the poet expressing joy, happiness, togetherness, friendship? Interpret the poem.

3. *Select the words you want to sign.* The signs for SATURDAY, RAIN, FRIEND, ME, and HAPPY might be picked.

4. *In the sign space, put the words in ASL order. Establish the time and place* (SATURDAY, RAIN). How long ago was this Saturday? Exactly where is it raining? Are these facts important? As the interpreter of the poem, you must decide these things. Sign the feeling last.

Here is a second poem to try. Follow the same steps.

### Umbrellas

*I like the many umbrellas,*
*All like wet tents*
*In the springtime rain*

90

1. *Create the picture in your mind.* Where is this taking place—a busy street, a country town, a schoolyard? What time of day is this happening? Does the time matter? Are people rushing around or walking leisurely? How many umbrellas are there? Are they big or small, and what colors? What do wet tents look like? Create as full a picture as you can. Use your imagination.

2. *Think about the poet's feelings.* Is the poet happy? What makes the poet happy? Do tents, springtime, or umbrellas cause the poet to think happy thoughts? Why? Interpret the poem. What does it mean to you?

3. *Select the particular words you want to sign.* You might choose MORNING, RAIN, SPRINGTIME, UMBRELLAS, MANY, and TENTS. Note that even though the word *morning* is not in the poem, the signer may choose to imagine that the scene is happening in the morning and therefore may sign MORNING.

MORNING

4. *In the sign space put the words in ASL order.* First establish the time, then the place (SPRINGTIME, MORNING). Where does the poet see the umbrellas? Then establish the action.

Here is one more haiku poem. Try signing it by yourself. In this book you will find all the signs you need to do it.

*Friend*

*A new school, what fun*
*Tomorrow I'll go early*
*I'll find a new friend*

Now you are ready to write and sign your own haiku.

SPRINGTIME

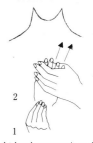

2

1

Right hand opens as it pushes up through left hand in "c" position. Repeat motion.

## SONGS

Although deaf people cannot hear music the way hearing people do, they are still able to participate in musical activities. Some hearing-impaired people, for example, are able to feel the rhythm of a song although they can't hear the actual notes. Signing songs helps to give some deaf people access to the beauty of music and hearing people access to the beauty of sign.

When a song is signed well, it reinforces the beat of the music. Unlike poetry, most words in a song should be signed,

COME HERE

and, like PSE, the words should be signed in the same order as they are sung. Finally, the words are mouthed—that is, shaped on the lips—in time to the rhythm of the music.

One well-known spiritual that children frequently enjoy either singing or signing is "Kum-Ba-Ya." The words mean "come here." The song is fun to sing because singers and signers can add verses to it simply by adding verbs. Here is the song. The sign for GOD is used instead of LORD, because the sign for LORD refers to a nobleman in a king's court, while the sign for GOD refers to God in heaven.

Kum ba ya my Lord (COME HERE MY GOD)
Kum ba ya (COME HERE)

(Repeat three times)

Oh Lord Kum ba ya (OH GOD COME HERE)

Someone's singing, Lord (SOMEONE SING GOD)
Kum ba ya (COME HERE)

(repeat three times)

Oh Lord Kum ba ya (OH GOD COME)

Other verbs can be substituted for SING. Here are some signs you already know: DRIVE, HOPE, SWIM, EAT, DANCE, and RIDE.

Musicians and sign language interpreters have arranged the music and words of many folk songs, patriotic songs, spirituals, and nursery rhymes in order that deaf people might enjoy them. Hearing people can also enjoy signing to music because it adds another measure of fun and appreciation to a familiar melody.

GOD

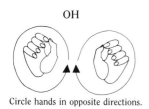

Right hand moves down in slight arcing motion from above the eyes.

OH

Circle hands in opposite directions.

SOMEONE

Index finger moves in small clockwise circle.

# Index

# About the Authors

Laura Greene is an English teacher and author. For Franklin Watts she has written several titles, including the original *Sign Language* book, *Computers in Business and Industry,* and *Pioneers in the Computer Industry.*

Eva Barash Dicker is an Interpreter Trainer at the University of Wisconsin–Milwaukee. She is a graduate of Gallaudet University in Washington, D.C., and has been "signing" all her life, for although she is a hearing person, both of her parents are deaf. She is a certified sign language instructor and interpreter and counsels deaf adults and children.